20 COMMON WRITING ERRORS

The purpose of this publication is to prepare students for the multiple choice questions on the Writing section of the PSAT and the SAT. Students need to become proficient with the grammar and usage rules most often tested on these exams.

Table of Contents

There are **20 Common Errors** tested on the SAT and PSAT.

Correct the error in each of the following sentences.
   A. Neither of the twins want to play football.
   B. He has finished writing his paper an hour ago.
   C. When Jean and Ellen arrive, tell her I'm ready.
   D. Sandy and Kate are trying on a bathing suit.
   E. My aunt left all of her jewelry to Anne and I.
   F. He was concerned with his chances of getting admitted to an Ivy League school.
   G. When I am sick, I love sitting by the fire, reading a good mystery, and I eat chicken soup.
   H. She ate too quick and then got a stomach ache.
   I.   The juniors at our school scored much higher on the PSAT than your school.
   J.   When Tim and John entered the classroom, I told him that he won.
   K. I woke up at 4 AM in the morning.
   L.   By attaining a perfect score on the SAT, my cousin achieved the goal that she set for herself.
   M. I didn't eat hardly any food at the party.
   N. The designer dress was located by the saleswoman with the beaded sash.
   O. While eating dinner, the fireworks startled me.
   P.   Did the committee ascent to your proposal?
   Q. The senators that signed the bill will have a tough time getting re-elected.
   R. If one wishes to be successful in life, you must have a good work ethic.
   S. Terry Bradshaw was one of the most successful NFL quarterbacks, he won three Super Bowls.
   T. The ball was hit into the stands by the batter.

Corrections and explanations of the above errors appear on the following pages.

A. **Neither of the twins want to play football.**
    Neither of the twins *wants* to play football.

SUBJECT-VERB AGREEMENT
Agreement means that a singular subject must be followed by a singular verb; a plural subject must be followed by a plural verb. Following are the RULES pertaining to subject-verb agreement.

1) A group of words often comes between the subject and the verb in the sentence. These words may form a phrase or a clause. A phrase is formed by a preposition, followed by a noun or a pronoun and any modifiers. A phrase may also be participial, formed by a participle and its modifiers (see pages 22-23). A clause contains a subject and a predicate and may be restrictive or non-restrictive (see page 26). The phrase or clause must be ignored when attempting to establish subject-verb agreement.

For a comprehensive list of prepositions see Appendix 1, page 35.

Ex. The last games of the tournament <u>are</u> being played on Friday.
Subject: games (plural)
Predicate: are being played (plural)

"Tournament" is part of the prepositional phrase "of the tournament" and, therefore, does not affect the subject-verb agreement.

2) Explanatory phrases, likewise do not affect the agreement of the subject and the verb.

Ex. My class, as well as all the other fifth grade classes, <u>was</u> guilty of rude behavior during the assembly.
Predicate: was (singular)
Subject: class (singular)

Ex. All of the boys, except John, <u>were</u> throwing things at the speaker.
Predicate: were throwing (plural)
Subject: All (plural)

3) Compound subjects joined by "and" are plural and take a plural verb.
Ex. Carol and Jenny <u>are</u> tied for first place in the ski-jump

4) A compound subject considered as a single unit takes a singular verb.
Ex. Peanut butter and jelly is my favorite sandwich.

5) Singular subjects joined by **or, nor, either...or, neither...nor** take a singular verb.
Ex. Neither John nor Phil <u>was</u> able to get tickets to the World Series.

6) When two subjects, one singular and the other plural, are joined by "or" or "nor" the verb agrees with the nearer subject.
Ex. Neither the teacher nor the students <u>were</u> pleased with the guest speaker.
Ex. Neither the students nor the teacher <u>was</u> pleased with the guest speaker.

7) Nouns that express quantities or amounts (e.g. time, money, weight, distance) usually take singular verbs.
Ex. Twenty pounds probably <u>represents</u> a reduction of at least two dress sizes.
Ex. Three miles a day <u>is</u> my limit.
Ex. A thousand dollars <u>is</u> a large investment for one so young.

8) The following indefinite pronouns usually take a singular verb: anyone, anybody, nobody, no one, neither, one, somebody, someone, everybody, everyone, either and each (even if an intervening phrase indicates a plural).

In <u>Cracking the SAT II: English</u>, Princeton Review authors, Buffa and Robinson, offer the following mnemonic device for this rule.
A anybody, anyone
N nobody, no one, neither
O one
S somebody, someone
E everybody, everyone, either, each
   You only have <u>one</u> nose; therefore, these words are singular.

9) The following indefinite pronouns may be either singular or plural: **some, most, all, any, none.** With these words, <u>the noun that the pronoun refers to in the phrase following the pronoun</u> indicates whether the word will take a singular or a plural verb.

Ex. Some of the boys <u>are</u> going to camp.
   "Boys" is plural; therefore, "some" in this sentence is plural and requires a plural verb, "are."
Ex. Some of the cake <u>was</u> left over.
    "Cake" is singular; therefore "some" in this sentence is singular and requires a singular verb.
Ex. Most of the movie <u>was</u> boring
    "Movie" is singular; therefore, "most" in this sentence is singular and requires a singular verb.
Ex. Most of my students <u>need</u> extra help to pass the test.
    "Students" is plural; therefore, "most" in this sentence is plural and requires a plural verb.
Ex. None of the freshmen <u>are</u> eligible to run for office.
    "Freshmen" is plural; therefore, "none" in this sentence is plural and requires a plural verb.
Ex. None of the report <u>was</u> actually <u>written</u> by Amy; her mother wrote all of it.
    "Report" is singular; therefore, "none" in this sentence is singular and requires a singular verb.

10) **Both, few, many, others** and **several** are plural indefinite pronouns and take a plural verb.
Ex. Few of the students were punished
Ex. Several of the boys are trying out for the two positions on the team.
Ex. Many of the new teachers are very young this year.
Ex. Others on the committee have decided not to vote.
Ex. Both of the dresses were out of stock

   It is essential for a writer to clarify the subject and the verb in a sentence before the above rules can be successfully incorporated into written, as well as oral, presentations.

Subject-Verb Agreement Practice
Underline the subject and circle the correct verb in the following sentences.

1. The last game of the series (take, takes) place on Friday.
2. The conflict between central government authority and individual states' rights (is, are) an endless battle.
3. The wedding pictures taken by my mother (look, looks) professionally done. ("taken by my mother" is a participial phrase)
4. The boat filled with food supplies and weapons (leave, leaves) soon. ("filled with food and supplies" is a participial phrase)
5. Weather conditions in the United States (vary, varies) greatly from region to region.
6. Her arguments against the planned trip (convince, convinces) me to change my plans.
7. One computer for three students (is, are) not enough.
8. Neither my sister nor my brothers (was, were) able to make it through the storm.
9. Spaghetti and meatballs (is, are) my favorite meal.
10. Some of the ice cream (was, were) left over.
11. John, who is my brother-in-law, (play, plays) professional football for the NY Giants. ("who is my brother-in-law" is a non-restrictive clause)
12. A weight loss of ten pounds (allow, allows) me to fit into a smaller dress size.
13. Some of the ice cream cones (is, are) melting.
14. Each of the students in the lab (is, are) responsible for (their, his) own equipment.
15. All of the football players, including my brother, (has, have) been put on probation for breaking the curfew rule.

B. He has finished writing his paper an hour ago.
He *finished* writing his paper an hour ago. Past tense or
He *has finished* writing his paper *already*. Present perfect tense
("already" indicates indefinite time)

VERB TENSE

Each verb places the action or state of being in the past, the present or the future. The verb form is called the tense.

Present	Past	Past Participle
Examples: eat	ate	eaten
go	went	gone
use	used	used

The past participle is used to form the present perfect tense and the past perfect tense which are the two tenses most often tested on the PSAT and the SAT.

The **present perfect tense** is used to express action that begins in the past and continues into the future.

Ex. I have taught for over thirty years.

The **present perfect tense** also expresses action that has been completed at an indefinite time. (See B above)

Ex. He has finished eating **already**. (already is an indefinite time)
He has seen that show **before**. (before is an indefinite time)

The **past perfect tense** is used to express action completed before another past action in the sentence.

Ex. I had taught for thirty years when I retired.

The action that comes first in the sentence is in the past perfect tense (had taught); the other action is in the past tense (retired).

The **future perfect tense** is used to express action that is completed before another future action. This tense is not often tested on the PSAT and SAT.

Ex. I **will have finished** painting before you arrive.

Avoid <u>unnecessary</u> tense shifts.

Once you use a verb in the past, present or future tense, keep the tense consistent throughout the sentence.

Incorrect:
Each time I **visit** Washington D.C., I **went** to the Air and Space Museum.
      (present)   (past)
Correct:
Each time I **visit** Washington D.C., I **go** to the Air and Space Museum.
      (present)   (present)
                              or
Each time I **visited** Washington D.C., I **went** to the Air and Space Museum.
      (past)   (past)

Use the **infinitive** (the infinitive is **to + the original form of the verb**) to express an action that follows another action.

Ex. John said that he hoped **to arrive** soon.
    Marcel wanted **to design** an award winning dress for the competition.

Verb Tense Practice

All of the tenses in the following sentences are used correctly. Explain the meaning of each sentence according to the tense used.

1. John has contributed stimulating ideas at every meeting of the committee

Ex. John has contributed ideas in the past and continues to do so.

_____

2. Sam had waited for three hours when the plane finally landed.

_____

3. Mr. Smith has been the moderator of the debate club for three years.

_____

4. Joe had coached the team for twenty years when he retired.

_____

5. He has finished his homework already.

_____

C. **When Jean and Ellen arrive, tell her I'm ready.**
   When Jean and Ellen arrive, tell *them* I'm ready.

PRONOUN-ANTECEDENT AGREEMENT

The **antecedent** is the noun or pronoun to which the pronoun refers. The pronoun must agree with its antecedent in number and gender.

1) The following indefinite pronouns are considered singular: **each, either, neither, one, everyone, everybody, no one, nobody, anyone, anybody, someone, somebody.** An intervening phrase does not change the fact that these antecedents are singular. (See Rule 8-Subject-Verb agreement, page 4)

Ex. **Each** of the women chose **her** own ensemble.
    One of the boys seemed excessively tall for **his** age.

2) A collective noun is singular in form but stands for a group of persons, animals or things, e.g. class, group, department, committee, audience, flock. A pronoun referring to one of these collective nouns would take the singular form.

Ex. The class achieved **its** goal of raising $1000.

3) Some words are plural in form but singular in usage (e.g. measles, civics, physics, mathematics).

Ex. When measles strikes an adult, **it** can be very serious.

Pronoun-Antecedent Agreement Practice
Circle the antecedent and write the correct pronoun in the blank.

1. Each of the boys has _____ own bicycle.
2. Neither my mother nor my sister has _____ hair done professionally.
3. Mr. Smith has done _____ share of the work.
4. The government has assisted the victims of the hurricane in getting _____ necessary supplies.
5. The fleet heard all the people on the shore cheer for _____ arrival.
6. The students finished _____ tests in time.
7. The class finished _____ project ahead of schedule.

D. Sandy and Kate are trying on a bathing suit.
Sandy and Kate are trying on bathing *suits*.

AGREEMENT OF NOUNS

Nouns must agree in number with the nouns to which they are referring. Two people need two things (one each): two jobs, two boyfriends, two books, etc.

Examples:
Joe Montana and Steve Young were inducted as **members** into the Football Hall of Fame.
Many of the basketball players on our team received **scholarships**.
Pam and Ellen have great **jobs**.

Agreement of Nouns Practice

Correct the nouns that do not agree in the following sentences.

1. More and more young men are entering education programs in college to train as a teacher.

2. Peggy and Barbara are my best friend.

3. John, Tom, and Sam have written their term paper.

4. Place the bunches of flowers in a different vase.

5. Since they serve as a model for future teachers, cooperating teachers should be selected for their expert teaching skills.

More practice:
Complete 1-10 in Appendix 4A, page 49 – review of rules A, B, C, D.

E. My aunt left all of her jewelry to Anne and I.
My aunt left all of her jewelry to Anne and *me*.

PRONOUN CASE

Singular

	Nominative	Objective	Possessive
1st person	I	me	my, mine
2nd person	you	you	your, yours
3rd person	he, she, it	him, her, it	his, hers, its
	who	whom	whose

Plural

	Nominative	Objective	Possessive
1st person	we	us	our, ours
2nd person	you	you	your, yours
3rd person	they	them	their, theirs
	who	whom	whose

Nominative case pronouns are used only as the subject or the predicate nominative of a sentence or clause.

Ex. **We** are planning to go to Mexico on Spring break. (Subject)

Ex. It was **I** who scored the winning goal. (Predicate nominative)

Objective case pronouns may be used as the object of a preposition, the indirect object and/or the direct object in a sentence.

Ex. The coach gave the game ball to **him.** (object of the preposition)

   The coach gave **him** the ball. (indirect object)

   The coach called **him**. (direct object)

Possessive case pronouns are adjectives that designate ownership. They must be used before a gerund (a verbal noun).

Ex. My going far away to college is very upsetting to my parents.

"Going" is the subject of the sentence; therefore, it is a verb being used as a noun – a gerund.

Pronoun Case Practice

Choose the correct pronoun.

1. The teacher gave (I, me) the answer.
2. The teacher about (who, whom) we were talking retired last year.
3. My husband was so excited about (my, me) winning the award.
4. (We, Us) students were waiting so long, we wondered what happened to (him, he).
5. After graduation, Tara and (she, her) want to live in the city.

F. He was concerned with his chances of getting admitted to an Ivy League school.
He was *concerned about* his chances of getting admitted to an Ivy League school.

IDIOMS

An idiom is an expression that requires a specific preposition to follow a particular word. The pairings follow convention rather than a set rule. Idioms must be memorized. Students need to familiarize themselves with the comprehensive list of idioms found in Appendix 2, pages 36-38.

Idiom Practice

Fill in the correct preposition.

1. The judge was indifferent _____ the criminal's repeated pleas for mercy.
2. The atmosphere in the day care center is conducive _____ creative play.
3. He was prevented _____ harming himself because he wore protective gear.
4. The professor demonstrated great insight _____ the meanings of Keat's poems.
5. The principal is responsible _____ the efficient running of the building.

G. When I am sick, I love sitting by the fire, reading a good mystery, and I eat chicken soup.
When I am sick, I love sitting by the fire, reading a good mystery, and *eating* chicken soup.

PARALLEL STRUCTURE

1) Items in a series need to be expressed in parallel grammatical form. A noun is paired with another noun, a phrase with a phrase, a clause with a clause, an infinitive with an infinitive, a participle with a participle.

Ex. Incorrect: During the summer, I love swimming, hiking and **to go boating**

  Revised: During the summer, I love swimming, hiking and **boating.**

  Incorrect: To achieve his success he devoted many years to intense research, extensive travel and **making contacts around the world**.

  Revised: To achieve his success he devoted many years to intense research, extensive travel and **worldwide contacts**.

2) Correlative conjunctions must be placed immediately before the parallel terms. The correlative conjunctions are **both…and, not only…but also, either…or, neither…nor, whether…or, just as…so.** These conjunctions are always used together in a sentence.

Ex. Incorrect: My grandfather **neither enjoyed reading nor listening** to music.

  Revised: My grandfather enjoyed **neither reading nor listening** to music.

  Incorrect: The hairdresser **did not only a great job** on the bride's hair, **but also** on all the bridesmaids' hair.

  Revised: The hairdresser did a great job **not only on the bride's hair but also on all the bridesmaids' hair.**

3) Repeat an article, a preposition, a noun, or a pronoun when repetition is necessary to clarify the meaning of the sentence.

Confusing: At the fund-raiser we were introduced to the principal and the director of the school. (Did we meet one person or two?)

Clear: At the fund-raiser we were introduced to the principal and **to** the director of the school. (We met two people.)

Confusing: The present that my dad received from his co-workers was just as appreciated by him as his boss. (Dad appreciated his boss and the present.)

Clear: The present that my dad received from his co-workers was just as appreciated by him as **the** gift from his boss. (Dad appreciated the gifts from his boss and from his co-workers.)

Parallel Structure Practice

Correct the faulty parallelism in the following sentences to make the meaning clear.

1. John lost the election because of his nasty temper and he spoke poorly.

_____

2. Thomas Hardy achieved success as an architect, a novelist and by writing poetry.

_____

3. My mom both experienced the joy of returning home and the sadness of realizing how many loved ones were missing.

_____

4. Jamie not only was a great soccer player but also an outstanding student.

_____

5. Today's menu listed fried chicken, baked fish and spare ribs that have been barbecued.

_____

_____

H. She ate too quick and then got a stomach ache.
   She ate too *quickly* and then got a stomach ache.

USE OF ADVERB OR ADJECTIVE?

An adjective may only describe, or modify a noun or a pronoun. An adjective tells **what kind, which one** or **how many**. An adjective may come before or after the noun or pronoun it modifies. An adjective is the more limited of the two parts of speech.

An adverb is more versatile. An adverb may describe, or modify a verb, an adjective or another adverb. An adverb tells, **how, when, where,** or **why**. An adverb may come <u>before or after</u> the verb it describes (ran quickly or quickly ran), but only <u>before</u> an adjective or adverb, e.g.. very pretty, very quickly.

On the writing sections of the PSAT and the SAT, you are usually asked to recognize an adjective that should be an adverb.

Note: "Good" is an adjective; "well" is an adverb.
   <u>Most</u> adverbs end in "ly"; some adverbs that do not end in "ly" are near, far, after, yesterday, today, tomorrow.

Adverb/Adjective Practice

Correct the adverb/adjective errors in the following sentences.

1. The baby smiled and quick grabbed the ice cream cone.
2. I answered the questions on the test easy.
3. It is amazing how close the statue resembles the living person.
4. You should do good on your SAT.
5. If you look at the prices close, you will see that the outlet stores do not always have the best prices.

More practice:
Complete 11-21 in Appendix 4B, pages 50-51–review of rules E, F, G, H.

I. **The juniors at our school scored higher on the PSAT than your school.**
The juniors at our school scored higher on the PSAT than *the juniors* at your school.

COMPARISONS

Of unlike objects:

When making a comparison, you must make clear what two things are being compared.
Incorrect: The population of New York City is greater than Albany.
(You cannot compare a population to a city.)
Correct: The population of New York City is greater than the population of Albany.
Incorrect: Skiing in Vermont is better than Colorado.
(You cannot compare skiing with Colorado.)
Correct: Skiing in Vermont is better than skiing in Colorado.

Make sure you are comparing nouns with nouns, actions with actions.
Remember: You cannot compare apples with oranges.

Use of comparative (er) and superlative (est) forms of adjectives

When you are comparing two things, use the comparative form.
Ex. Which twin is tall**er**?
Today is cold**er** than yesterday.

When you compare three or more things use the superlative form;

Ex. Alaska is the larg**est** state in the United States.
Ellen is the pretti**est** girl in the class.
Kevin is the tall**est** boy on the team.

Avoid double comparisons: more + the comparative form of the adjective

or

most + the superlative form of the adjective.

    Incorrect: Chocolate ice cream is more better than vanilla ice cream.
    Correct: Chocolate ice cream is better than vanilla ice cream.

    Incorrect: Sarah is the most happiest person I know.
    Correct: Sarah is the happiest person I know.

Add the word **other** or **else** when comparing one thing with a group of which it is a part.

    Incorrect: James is smarter than anyone in his class.
        (This means that James is smarter than himself.)
    Correct: James is smarter than anyone else in his class.

or

    James is smarter than any other student in his class.

Comparison Practice

Rewrite the following sentences, correcting the faulty comparison in each.

1. The seats in the orchestra are always more expensive than the balcony.

_____

2. Diane is the prettiest of the two girls I am dating.

_____

3. Swimming in a lake is more fun than the ocean.

_____

4. In the United States, the consumption of gasoline is greater than European countries.

_____

5. Rhode Island is smaller than any state in the United States.

_____

J. When Tim and John entered the classroom, I told him that he won.
When Tim and John entered the classroom, I told *Tim* that he was
the winner.

AMBIGUITY / INDEFINITE REFERENT

Ambiguity occurs when a pronoun can refer to two antecedents and the
reader does not know which antecedent is intended.
1) Watch pronouns carefully. Make sure they agree in number
(singular/plural) with their antecedent
Ex. Confusing: When the car hit the garage **it** was badly damaged.
    Was the car badly damaged or was the garage badly damaged?
    It is ambiguous in this sentence.
Clear: The garage was badly damaged when the car hit it.

Ex. Confusing: Mom told Jenny that **she** had to clean the house.
    Who has to clean the house, Mom or Jenny?
    She is ambiguous in this sentence.
Clear: Mom told Jenny that Jenny had to clean the house.

Ambiguity Practice

Correct the ambiguity in the following sentences. Make each sentence clear.

1. As he drove his car up to the ATM machine, it made a strange sound.

_____

_____

2. The teacher explained to the student the meaning of the poem she had
read.

_____

_____

3. Jim told Gary that his expenses would be much greater when he went to
college.

_____

_____

2) Avoid a reference that is vague.

       This type of error occurs when a pronoun refers confusingly to an idea within the sentence.

The pronouns **which, this, that** and **it** most commonly lead to ambiguity errors. These pronouns should be avoided when writing your essay.

Ex. Confusing: Many of our young adults leave their suburban homes to
                work in New York City, which is a pity.

    What is a pity - leaving their suburban homes **or** working in New York City?

Clear: It is a pity that many of our young adults leave the suburbs to work
      in New York City.

Ex. Confusing: My folks had their new beach house painted, redecorated,
             and landscaped professionally, which was very expensive.

    Which was expensive –the painting, the redecorating, or the landscaping?

Clear: It was very expensive for my parents to have their new beach house
      painted, redecorated and landscaped by professionals.

Ex. Confusing: We served our guests fettuccini Alfredo, chicken cordon
             bleu, and broccoli casserole. This was very fattening.

    Which part of the meal was fattening? or Was the whole meal fattening?

Clear: We served our guests a very fattening meal consisting of fettuccini
      Alfredo, chicken cordon bleu, and broccoli casserole.

More Ambiguity Practice

Correct the ambiguity in the following sentences.

4. The day of our planned picnic started off cold, became cloudy and ended in pouring rain, which brought about our gloomy mood.

_____

_____

5. The brave platoon fought the enemy until they were all captured.

_____

_____

K. **I woke up at 4 AM in the morning.**
   I woke up at *4 AM*. or I woke up at *4 o'clock in the morning.*
   (AM means "in the morning.")

.

REDUNDANCY

If you can remove words in the sentence without changing the meaning of the sentence, then these words are redundant.

Ex. Redundant: In my opinion, I think that we should go on vacation now.
Clear and concise: I think that wc should go on vacation now.

Ex. Redundant: Repeat those directions again.
Clear and concise: Repeat those directions.

Redundancy Practice

Rewrite the following sentences in a more concise way.

1. I watched the window washer descend down the building.

_____

_____

2. In the year of 1968, protestors of the Vietnam War were all over New York City.

_____

_____

3. The period of time from Thanksgiving to Christmas is one of the busiest shopping seasons of the year.

_____

_____

4. The consensus of opinions of this committee is that a new high school is not needed at this time.

_____

_____

5. The real fact is that there was not enough evidence to bring about an indictment.

_____

_____

L. **By attaining a perfect score on the SAT, my cousin achieved the goal that she set for herself.**
(A goal is something that one sets.)
By attaining a perfect score on the SAT, my cousin achieved *her goal.*

WORDINESS

A wordy sentence has words and phrases that add nothing to its meaning. Good writing is concise and to the point; it does not utilize extraneous words.

Examples:
Wordy: A thrifty person can redecorate a room, using little money or not spending any money at all.
Concise: A thrifty person can redecorate a room, using little or no money.

Wordy: The first person to recognize the potential that my sister showed for music was Mrs. Elison who was Clare's fifth grade special education teacher.
Concise: Mrs. Elison, my sister Clare's fifth grade special education teacher, was the first person to recognize Clare's musical talent.

Wordy: For at least as many as ten years, and probably more, my neighbor kept the fact of his real identity a secret.
Concise: For more than ten years, my neighbor kept his real identity a secret.

Wordy: Due to the fact that James did not get a high school diploma, he is finding it difficult to find a good job.
Concise: James is finding it difficult to get a good job because he did not get a high school diploma.

Wordy: The reason that I am studying so hard is because I need a scholarship to go to college.
Concise: I am studying hard because I need a scholarship to go to college.

***On the sections of the PSAT and the SAT where you are asked to select the wording that will produce the most effective sentence, you can usually eliminate the two longest choices (as measured by a ruler). In most cases, your answer will be one of the three shortest answer choices (as measured by a ruler). On these sections, if you are in doubt, pick short!!!!

More practice:
Complete 22-30 in Appendix 4C, pages 52-53 – review of rules I, J, K, L.

M. I didn't hardly eat any food at the party.
    I *hardly ate* any food at the party.

DOUBLE NEGATIVE

Two negative words cancel each other out. If I **didn't** eat **hardly** any food at the party, then I probably ate a lot of food at the party. Don't use two negative words when one is sufficient.

Watch out for these double negatives: can't hardly, can't scarcely, can't help but, haven't only, don't have no, isn't nothing, can't none.

Examples:
Incorrect: We don't have no money to spare.
Correct: We don't have any money to spare.

Incorrect: There isn't nothing I love more than chocolate.
Correct: There isn't anything I love more than chocolate.

Incorrect: Can't none of them come to the party?
Correct: Can't any of them come to the party?

Double Negative Practice

Rewrite the following sentences, eliminating the double negative.

1. We couldn't see hardly anything in front of us.

_____

2. I have no doubt but that Kevin will be elected president of the class.

_____

3. I can't hardly believe what you are telling me.

_____

N. The designer dress was located by the saleswoman with the beaded sash.
The designer *dress with the beaded sash* was located by the saleswoman.

MISPLACED MODIFIER

To avoid a misunderstanding — Is the beaded sash on the designer dress or on the saleswoman? – place a modifying word, phrase or clause as close as possible to the word or words they modify.
Examples:
Confusing: We cheered the winning team as they rode in open cars waving school banners.
Who was waving school banners – we **or** the team?
Clear: Waving school banners, we cheered the winning team as they rode in open cars.
We were waving school banners.
Confusing: I chased the robbers down the block dressed in my pajamas.
Is "the block" dressed in pajamas?
Clear: Dressed in my pajamas, I chased the robbers down the block.
The block wasn't dressed in my pajamas. I was.

Misplaced Modifier Practice
Make the following sentences clear by placing the modifiers near the words they modify.

1. My father shot the deer creeping near our flowerbeds with his new rifle.

_____

2. They are looking for a larger house for their growing family with six bedrooms.

_____

3. The man carried the huge carton down the stairs grumbling all the time.

_____

4. The crime scene investigators found the body in a small ravine disappointed after the long search.

_____
_____

O. While eating dinner, the fireworks startled me.
  While *I* was eating dinner, the fireworks startled me.

DANGLING MODIFIER

There must be a word in the sentence that a descriptive phrase or clause can modify clearly and sensibly. If there is no word that the phrase or clause can sensibly modify, the modifier is described as "dangling."
The word "I" clearly shows who was eating dinner.

Examples:
Confusing: Carrying a load of boxes, the stairway was difficult to climb.
   Clear: Carrying a load of boxes, I had a difficult time climbing the stairway.
A change of subject eliminates the dangling participle.

Confusing: Enchanted by the special effects, the movie was one of the best I had ever seen.
   Clear: Enchanted by the special effects, I thought that the movie was one of the best I had ever seen.
A change of subject eliminates the dangling participle.

Confusing: At the age of seven, Julie's dad took her to Disneyworld.
   Clear: When Julie was seven, her dad took her to Disneyworld.
Changing the adjective phrase to an adverb clause eliminates the dangling phrase.

Dangling Modifier Practice

Rewrite the following sentences to correct the dangling modifier.

1. Walking home in the snowstorm, our shoes got soaked.

   _____

2. Deer and pheasants were seen driving through Seven Lakes Drive.

   _____

3. The rain changed from a slow drizzle to a raging downpour looking out the window.

   _____

   _____

P. Did the committee ascent to your proposal?
    Did the committee *assent* to your proposal?

WORDS COMMONLY CONFUSED

Sometimes a writer or speaker must choose between two words to effectively communicate his meaning. These words **may** sound the same but be spelled differently, or the words are entirely different, but their meanings are confused.

Refer to the list of commonly confused words in Appendix 3, pages 39-48.

Following are a few examples. Consult Appendix 3 before attempting the practice drill.
Ex. I ate fewer ice cream cones than you did.
    I ate less ice cream than you did.
       Explanation: Use **fewer** for items that can be counted (cones).
                        Use **less** for a quantity that cannot be counted (ice cream).
Ex. Milton included many classical allusions in his poetry.
    Anne was under the illusion for years that Tim was going to marry her.
    Explanation: An **allusion** is a reference to a well-known person, place, thing or idea. An **illusion** is a false or misleading idea.

Commonly Confused Words Practice
Underline the correct word choice. Be sure to study Appendix 3.

1. I had to choose (between, among) the two gowns.
2. You must fill out some papers at the (personal, personnel) office before your interview for the job.
3. The temperatures in the (desert, dessert) often exceed 100 degrees.
4. The upholstery was too (coarse, course), and it made the couch uncomfortable.
5. Place the new end table (beside, besides) the sofa.

Show your understanding of the correct usage of the following words by writing a sentence for each: affect, effect, accept, except, amount, number, principal (as an adjective and as a noun), principle, bring, take.

More practice:
Complete 31-36 in Appendix 4D, page 54- review of rules M, N, O, P.

Q. The senators that signed the bill will have a tough time getting re-elected.

The senators *who* signed the bill will have a tough time getting re-elected.

CORRECT USE OF WHO, WHICH, and THAT

Who, which and **that** are relative pronouns used to introduce dependent clauses. A dependent clause is a group of words containing a subject and a verb, but it cannot stand alone as a complete thought.

Who refers to a **single person** or to a **group thought of as individuals** (e.g. senators, jurors, players). **Which** refers to animals and things. Use **that** or **which** for a collective noun thought of as a single entity (the senate **that**, the team **which**)
The difference between **which** and **who** is <u>consistently</u> tested on the SAT.
The difference between **which** and **that** has <u>rarely</u> been tested.

Who or **that** may be used to introduce a restrictive clause (a clause that *is essential* to the meaning of the sentence – see examples 1, 2, and 3). A restrictive clause is ***not*** set off by commas. A non-restrictive clause (one that *is not essential* to the meaning of the sentence – see example 4) is introduced by **which** and ***is*** set off by commas.

Examples:
 (restrictive clause)
1. The students (**who** failed the English Regents) must take a language arts support class next year.
    The clause is restrictive because, if it is dropped, then **all** students must take a language support class next year.
 (restrictive clause)
2. The courses (**that** are required for graduation) are listed in the student handbook.
    The clause is restrictive because if it is dropped then **all** the courses are listed in the handbook and it would not be clear which ones are required for graduation.

(restrictive clause)

3. Children (**who** are allergic to peanuts) must check the ingredients on every candy bar before eating it.

    Not every child must check the ingredients on a candy bar, only those "who are allergic to peanuts;" therefore, the clause if restruitive.

(non-restrictive clause)

4. The tickets for the Tim McGraw concert, (**which** went on sale yesterday), are already sold out

    The fact that "the tickets went on sale yesterday" is not vital information. This clause can be dropped from the sentence without losing anything of importance; therefore, the clause is non-restrictive.

Who-Which-That Practice

Choose the correct pronoun in the following sentences.

1. There is not enough food for the guests (who, which) have already arrived.
2. Tragic stories often have a particular fascination for those people (who, which) have experienced their own personal traumas.
3. The girl (who, which) came in first in the race is my sister.
4. The cost of $660 for the lecture series, (which, that) reflects a 10% increase over last year's fee, will be sufficient to cover the additional overhead.
5. The team (who, which, that) won the World Series is the Chicago White Sox.

R. **If one wishes to be successful in life, you must have a good work ethic.**

If *one* wishes to be successful in life, *one* must have a good work ethic.

or

If *you* wish to be successful in life, *you* must have a good work ethic.

PRONOUN SHIFT

Pronouns within a sentence, referring to the same person, must be consistent in form.

Example:
Incorrect: When **you** view the sun rising over the ocean, **one** is truly awed by the magnificence of nature.

Correct: When **one** views the sun rising over the ocean, **one** is truly awed by the magnificence of nature.

Pronoun Shift Practice

Correct the incorrect pronoun in each of the following sentences.

1. If one wishes to be an Olympic skater, you must be willing to practice for many hours each day.
2. You need to take many advanced placement courses during your junior and senior years, if one wishes to get into a more prestigious college.
3. If a teacher wants to be liked, you have to treat all students with fairness and respect.
4. Students should do their homework on a nightly basis, so that your workload doesn't overwhelm them.

S. **Terry Bradshaw was one of the most successful NFL quarterbacks, he won three Super Bowls.**
Terry Bradshaw was one of the most successful NFL quarterbacks; he won three Super Bowls.
The use of a semi-colon corrects the run-on sentence.

SENTENCE STRUCTURE – Run-ons and Fragments

When two complete thoughts are not separated by a period (.) or a semi-colon (;), or a comma and a conjunction, the result is a run-on sentence. A comma alone (,) indicates a pause but is not strong enough to separate two complete thoughts.

A run-on sentence consists of two independent clauses, connected incorrectly. Each clause "Terry Bradshaw was one of the most successful NFL quarterbacks" and "he won three Super Bowls" could stand alone as a complete thought containing a subject and a predicate. When clauses such as these are not separated by a period (.), a semi-colon (;), or a comma and a conjunction (and, or, but, nor) the result is a run on sentence.

A semi-colon can be used to correct the run-on because a semi-colon may correctly connect two, closely related, independent clauses without the use of a conjunction.

Ex. Fall is my favorite season; it is so colorful.
    Paul loves to play golf; however, he rarely finds the time to play.

A sentence fragment is a group of words that does not have a subject and a predicate which express a complete thought.

Fragment: Terry Bradshaw one of the most successful NFL quarterbacks.
           This "sentence" lacks a verb.
Complete sentence: Terry Bradshaw **is** one of the most successful NFL
           quarterbacks.
           "Is" is a verb.

Sentence Structure Practice

Rewrite each of the following sentence fragments to make each of them into a complete sentence; correct the run-on sentences by using correct punctuation or adding a conjunction.

1. After the game was over.

_____

2. The committee met for hours nothing was accomplished.

_____

3. My time in London was too short I hardly saw all the sites I had read about.

_____

4. The very room where the group held its meetings.

_____

5. My mother bailed furiously the waves continued to pour more water into our floundering craft.

_____

T. The ball was hit into the stands by the batter.
   (The subject of the sentence _is not_ the doer of the action - passive)
   The batter hit the ball into the stands.
   (The subject of the sentence _is_ the doer of the action – active)

ACTIVE VOICE/PASSIVE VOICE

A verb is in the **active voice** when the doer of the action (batter) is the subject of the sentence.
A verb is in the **passive voice** when the subject of the sentence (ball) is not the **doer** of the action but the **receiver** of the action (was hit).
The Passive Voice always includes part of the verb "to be" (be, am, is, was, were, has, have or had been).
***When given a choice in the sections of the PSAT and SAT that require you to revise the sentence, always choose the active voice. A choice written in the active voice is most often shorter than the choice utilizing passive voice. Active voice is a less wordy, more concise, more effective form of speech.
Passive voice is acceptable when the doer of the action is unknown or unimportant.
Ex. It has been said that women who smoke during their pregnancy will deliver smaller babies than women who do not smoke during their pregnancy.

Active/Passive Voice Practice
If the sentence is in the passive voice, rewrite it in the active voice.

   1. The Mona Lisa was painted by Da Vinci.
   _____

   2. Many changes to my research paper were suggested by my professor.
   _____

   3. Our dog ate all of the leftovers from the party.
   _____

   4. Pam gave me a beautiful silk scarf.
   _____

   5. America was discovered by Columbus.
   _____

More practice:
Complete 37-43 in Appendix 4E, page 55 – review of rules Q, R, S, T.

COMMON ERRORS – ANSWER KEY

Page 5-Subject-verb agreement

1. takes	10. was
2. is	11. plays
3. look	12. allows
4. leaves	13. are
5. vary	14. is, his
6. convince	15. have
7. is	
8. were	
9. is	

Page 7- Tense drill

1. John contributed ideas in the past and continues to contribute ideas today.
2. Sam's waiting was over when the plane landed.
3. Mr. Smith was the moderator of the club for the past three years and still is.
4. When Joe retired, his twenty years of coaching was completed.
5. "Already" represents an indefinite time, so the present perfect tense is used.

Page 8-Pronoun-antecedent agreement

1. his
2. her
3. his
4. their
5. its
6. their
7. its

Page 9-Agreement of Nouns

1. to train as teachers
2. my best friends
3. term papers
4. different vases
5. as models

Page 10-Pronoun case

1. me
2. whom
3. my
4. We, him
5. she

Page 11- Idioms

1. indifferent to
2. conducive to
3. prevented from
4. insight into
5. responsible for

Page 13-Parallel structure

1. Joe lost the election because he had a nasty temper and poor speaking ability.
2. Thomas Hardy achieved success as an architect, a novelist, and a poet.
3. My mom experienced both the joy of returning home and the sadness of realizing how many loved ones were missing.
4. Jamie was not only a great soccer player but also an outstanding student.
5. Today's menu listed fried chicken, baked fish and barbecued spare ribs.

Page 14- Adverb-adjective
1. quickly
2. easily
3. closely
4. well
5. closely

Page 16-Comparisons
1. The seats in the orchestra are always more expensive than the seats in the balcony .
2. Diane is the prettier of the two girls I am dating.
3. Swimming in a lake is more fun than swimming in the ocean.
4. In the United States, the consumption if gasoline is greater than the consumption of gas in European countries.
5. Rhode Island is smaller than any other state in the United States.

Page 17-Ambiguity
1. As he drove his car up to the ATM machine, the car made a strange sound.
2. The teacher explained the meaning of the poem she had read to her student.
3. Jim told Gary that Gary's expenses would be much greater when Gary went to college.

Page 18-More Ambiguity
4. Our gloomy mood began when the day of our planned picnic started off cold, became cloudy, and ended in pouring rain.
5. The brave platoon fought the enemy until the enemy forces were all captured.

Page 19-Redundancy
1. I watched the window washer descend the building.
2. In 1968, protestors of the Vietnam War were all over New York City.
3. The period between Thanksgiving and Christmas is one of the busiest shopping seasons.
4. The consensus of this committee is that a new high school is not needed at this time.
5. The fact is that there was not enough evidence to indict.

Page 21-Double Negative
1. We could see only a few inches in front of us.
2. I have no doubt that Kevin will be elected president of the class.
3. I can hardly believe what you are telling me.

Page 22-Misplaced Modifier
1. With his new rifle, my father shot the deer creeping near our flowerbeds.
2. They are looking for a larger house with six bedrooms for their growing family.
3. Grumbling all the time, the man carried the huge carton down the stairs.
4. Disappointed after their long search, the crime scene investigators found the body in a small ravine.

Page 23-Dangling Modifier
1. Our shoes got soaked when we walked home in the snowstorm.
2. When we were driving through Seven Lakes Drive, we saw deer and pheasants.
3. While we were looking out the window, the rain changed from a slow drizzle to a raging downpour.

Page 24-Commonly Confused Words
1. between
2. personnel
3. desert
4. coarse
5. beside
Answers will vary.

Page 26-Who-Which-That
1. who
2. who
3. who
4. which
5. that

Page 27-Pronoun shift
1. you>one
2. one>you
3. you have>he/she has
4. your>their

Page 29-Sentence Structure
Answers will vary.

Page 30-Active/Passive Voice
1. Da Vinci painted the Mona Lisa.
2. My professor suggested many changes to my research paper.
3. Active voice
4. Active voice
5. Columbus discovered America.

Prepositions – Appendix 1

about	throughout
above	to
across	toward
after	under
against	until
along	up
among	with
around	
at	
before	
behind	
beside	
between	
beyond	
by	
down	
during	
except	
for	
from	
in	
into	
like	
near	
of	
off	
on	
over	
past	
through	

Abound in (or with)- This letter abounds in mistakes.

Absorbed in- My dad was so absorbed in his work, he never heard us come into the room.

Accompanied by (a person)- The salesman was accompanied by the buyer.

Accompanied with (a gift)- He accompanied the closing of the contract with a gift.

Acquit of -The manager was acquitted of the charges against him.

Adept at (or in)- He is adept at typing.

Agree to (an offer)- The firm agreed to the settlement of the claim.

Agree upon (or on) (a plan)- We must agree upon the best method.

Agree with (a person)- We must agree with the counselor's opinion.

Angry about (an event, situation)- I am very angry about the decision.

Angry with (a person)- The boss was extremely angry with the workers.

Angry at (a thing, an animal)- He was angry at the dog.

Appropriate for (meaning suitable to)- Her gown is appropriate for the prom.

Argued about- They argued about the money for hours.

Arrested for- She was arrested for shoplifting again.

Available for (a purpose)- The doctor is available for a consultation now.

Available to (a person)- What solution is available to you at this time?

Averse to- The President is averse to a tax increase.

Capable of- He was capable of achieving much higher scores.

Caused by- The rash was caused by the rough material.

Cognizant of- He was not cognizant of dissension among his workers.

Coincide with- Your wishes coincide with mine.

Commensurate with- Your success will be commensurate with your effort.

Commitment to- You have a commitment to complete your obligations.

Compare to (shows similarity between things that have different forms)-
In one sonnet, Shakespeare compares a woman's hair to wire.

Compare with (shows similarity or difference between things of like form)-
The assignment is to compare Thoreau's essays with Emerson's.

Compatible with- The aims of the management should be compatible with those of the employees.

Comply with- If you do not wish to comply with the rules, you may leave.

Concerned about- I was concerned about my grades.

Conducive to– The atmosphere in the office is conducive to good work.

Conform to- The average person conforms to the vote of the majority.

Conversant with- We need a salesman who is fully conversant with the product he is selling.

Desirous of- We are not desirous of a price increase.

Different from- This machine is different from the old one.

Indifferent to- I am indifferent to your promises.

Differ from (a thing in appearance)- A coat differs from a cape.

Differ with (an opinion)- I differ with your political views.

Dissuade from- She will dissuade him from taking that course of action.

Employed at (a definite salary)- A student aide is employed at the minimum wage.

Employed in (certain work)- His brother is employed in computer sales.

Employed by (a company)- He is employed by H&R Block.

Envious of- Some of his relatives are envious of his good fortune.

Far away from (indicates distance)- He was far away from the scene of the accident when it occurred.

Far from (indicates contrast)- Far from being the conservative leader we thought he would be, Farley actually introduced some very progressive programs.

Focused on- It was impossible to focus on my studies with all the noise.

Helpful for- These tools will be helpful for the project.

Identical to (or with)- These socks are identical to the ones I bought last week.

In accordance with- You must act in accordance with the regulations.

In contrast to- In contrast to her sisters, Jenna is much more agreeable.

Inconsistent with- The evidence was inconsistent with the student's account of the story.

Indebted to- I will be indebted to you for the rest of my life.

Infer from- I could infer from his remarks that he was angry.

In search of- Columbus set out in search of fame and fortune.

Insight into- The doctor showed great insight into the patient's problems.

Necessary to (or for)- Your cooperation is necessary for the success of the project.

Oblivious of (or to)- The students were oblivious to the noise from the construction.

One of its kind- This gem is the only one of its kind in the world.

Opposite to (or from) (position)- He sat opposite to the judge.

Opposition to (or with) (opinion)- My views are in total opposition to yours.

Pertinent to- That information is not pertinent to this discussion.

Prefer to- She prefers silk to rayon. They prefer to walk rather than to ride.

Preoccupied with- I was so preoccupied with the details of the party, that I did not enjoy myself.

Prevent from- He was prevented from jumping by the fireman's quick actions.

Prior to- You will receive the tickets prior to the performance.

Prohibit from- He was prohibited from smoking on the premises.

Regarded as- He is regarded as an expert in his field.

Required of (a person)- The letter states the responsibilities that will be required of you.

Required to (a verb)- The letter states the duties that you will be required to complete.

Responsible for (something)- The Secret Service is responsible for the safety of the President.

Responsible to (a person)- The Cabinet members are responsible to the President.

Solution for- They committee is hoping to reach a solution for the problem.

Tendency to- My dad has a tendency to exaggerate when he is telling a story.

Vie with- The salesmen are vying with each other for the trip to Hawaii.

APPENDIX 3

USAGE ERRORS: CONFUSED OR MISUSED WORDS

accept
(verb) to receive
Maria *accepted* John's invitation to dinner.

except
(preposition) other than
All the boys *except* Jason are avid Mets fans.

advice
(noun) counsel
His *advice* was very helpful.

advise
(verb) to give advice
He *advised* me to meet with my teacher after class.

affect
(verb) to influence
Hurricane Katrina *affected* the price of gasoline in our country.

effect
(verb) to cause or bring about; to accomplish
The new principal has *effected* many new changes in the school.
(noun) the result
The *effect* of the crisis is being felt at all levels of government.

allowed
(verb) permitted; let happen
The children weren't *allowed* to have dessert.

aloud
(adverb) in a normal voice
Don't speak *aloud* during the performance.

allusion
(noun) a passing reference or mention of historical or fictional characters, places or events
William Shakespeare's plays are filled with *allusions* to the Bible and mythology.

illusion
(noun) a false impression or idea.
A magician's performance is based on creating *illusions* to awe his audience.

allude
(verb) to make a reference to
Shakespeare *alludes* to mythology in many of his plays.

elude
(verb) to escape from
The thief *eluded* the police.

a lot	not one word: a lot (two words) means "a portion of land." The phrase *a lot* should not be used in formal writing.
allot	(verb) to divide or distribute by share or portion Our school allotted four tickets per senior for the graduation ceremony this year.
already	(adverb) tells when. Are you finished *already*?
all ready	(adjective phrase) completely ready The players were *all ready* to board the bus.
all right	(adjective phrase) correct or satisfactory (alright is not a word)
altogether	(adverb) completely Jane was *altogether* wrong.
all together	(phrase) used to describe people or things which are gathered in one place at one time The non-swimmers were *all together* in the shallow end of the pool.
among	(preposition) used when discussing more than two persons or things The students quarreled *among* themselves.
between	(preposition) used when discussing only two There was a fence *between* the two houses.
amount	(noun) used when referring to things that can be weighed or measured, but not counted What *amount* of shortening is needed in this recipe?
number	(noun) used when the quantity can be counted You would be surprised at the *number* of calories in one cookie.
annual	(adjective) occurs once every year Mrs. Rodriquez attends an *annual* teachers' conference.
biannual	**(adjective)** occurs twice every year A *biannual* or *semiannual* event occurs twice every year
perennial	(noun and adjective) lasts throughout the year or over many years We landscaped our property with *perennials*. (noun) Finding reliable employees is a perennial problem. (adjective)

biennial	(adjective) occurs every second year or lasts for two years
ante	prefix meaning "before" or "in front of" An *antechamber* is a small room just before a main room.
anti	prefix meaning "opposed to" or "against" *Anti-American* sentiment is a growing problem around the world.
ascent	(noun) the act of rising The plane's steep *ascent* frightened the passengers.
assent	(verb) to agree The accused *assented* to a guilty plea. (noun) agreement She nodded her *assent* when invited to come.
beside	(preposition) next to; apart from Joan placed her bag *beside* the chair.
besides	(adverb) in addition to; moreover; furthermore *Besides* paying Mark's college tuition, his parents also had to pay off his car loan.
brake	(noun) a device for slowing or stopping the motion of a wheel or vehicle. It is important that the *brakes* of the car are checked.
break	(verb) to split, crack, or destroy A person of integrity tries to never *break* a promise..
bring	(verb) used when the action is moving toward the speaker Please *bring* me the empty platter.
take	(verb) used when the action is moving away from the speaker *Take* the filled platter out to our guests.
can	able to *Can* the baby have solid foods yet?
may	permitted to *May* I borrow your car?

capital	(noun) refers to a city or money
	Albany is the *capital* of New York State.
	Taxes provide the *capital* needed to run the country.
	(adjective) major or important; referring to the death penalty
	Murder is a capital offense in some states.
capitol	(noun) refers to a building.
	Congress conducts its sessions in the *Capitol*.
choice	(noun) a selection
	Selecting Mike as captain of the team was a wise *choice*.
	(adjective) excellent; carefully selected
	The guest of honor was given a *choice* seat at the reception.
chose	(verb) past tense of "to choose"
	Because Bill *chose* to eat a banana split following a huge lunch, he will choose to skip dinner tonight.
cite	(verb) to quote
	The defense attorney *cited* the Bill of Rights in his closing statement.
sight	(noun) vision or what is seen
	The sun setting over the ocean is a beautiful *sight*.
site	(noun) the place where something is located or occurs
	The *site* for the town pool has been approved.
coarse	(adjective) rough or crude
	The *coarse* fabric made the jeans uncomfortable.
course	(noun) a path or direction taken
	The ship went off *course* in the storm.
	(noun) a class
	Molly loved her photography *course*.
complement	(verb) to complete or bring to perfection
	The white couch *complements* the modern décor in the room.
compliment	(verb) to say something flattering
	Maria's teacher *complimented* her on her well-written essay.
	(noun) a flattering or praising remark
	The *compliment* embarrassed Maria.

continual (adjective) of regular recurrence; very frequent
The *continual* bus departures from the Port Authority make commuting to the city easy.

continuous (adjective) uninterrupted
The *continuous* noise and disruptions in class make learning almost impossible.

consul (noun) the representative of a foreign country
The Italian *consul* was a guest at the White House.

council (noun) a group that advises
A *council* of physicians met to decide on the best course of action in the event of a flu epidemic.

councilor (noun) a member of a council
One of the *councilors* abstained from voting on the proposal.

counsel (noun) advice
His *counsel* was most helpful.
(verb) to advise
The attorney *counseled* his client to accept a plea bargain.

counselor (noun) one who gives advice
The school guidance *counselor* is a student advocate.

decent (adjective) suitable
The *decent* thing to do is to return the lost dog to its owner.

descent (noun) the act of going down
The *descent* into the dark cave frightened the children.

dissent (verb) to differ in opinion
He *dissented* with his peers on the question of changing the legal drinking age.
(noun) disagreement
She noted the *dissent* among the disgruntled workers.

desert (noun) a barren wilderness
Cactus grows readily in the *desert*.

desert (verb) to abandon
Matt *deserted* his friends when they needed him.

dessert (noun) food served after a meal
My favorite *dessert* is rice pudding.

farther	(adverb) used to express distance
	Florida is *farther* south than Bermuda.
further	(adjective) additional
	The police attempted to get *further* information from the witnesses.
fewer	(adjective) refers to things that can be counted
	I have *fewer* pieces of candy than you.
less	(adjective) refers to bulk quantity (can't be counted)
	You have *less* money than I.
good	(adjective) the opposite of bad
	Mr. Jones is a *good* teacher.
well	(almost always an adverb) in a skillful manner
	The children in his class learn their lessons *well*.
	(adjective) healthy
	Ms. Jones was absent yesterday because she didn't feel *well*.
	Usage note: To feel good and to feel well mean different things. To feel *good* means to feel happy or pleased. To feel *well* means to feel healthy.
	Linda feels *good* about her grades this semester. Matt went to the nurse because he didn't feel *well* after seeing his grades.
immigrate	(verb) to come into a new country
	Many people *immigrated* to the United States at the beginning of the 20th century.
emigrate	(verb) to go out of one country to live in another
	Most of them *emigrated* from western Europe.
formally	(adverb) properly, according to strict rules
	The guest lecturer was *formally* introduced.
formerly	(adverb) previously, in the past
	He was *formerly* the ambassador to Italy.
it's	contraction for "it is"
	It's time to leave for school.
its	(possessive pronoun) must be followed by a noun
	The bee stopped *its* buzzing.

knew	(verb) the past tense of "to know"
	The graduate *knew* that life would be different following his commencement.
new	(adjective) recent or modern
	His life would be filled with many *new* challenges.
know	(verb) to understand
	She *knows* the difference between right and wrong.
no	(adverb) the opposite of yes
	No, that's not right.
	(adjective) not any
	He made *no* mistakes.
later	(adverb) after a period of time
latter	(adjective) the second of two mentioned
	Later that day I met two friends, John and Jean; the *latter* has been my friend since grammar school.
lead	(verb) to guide
	Bill will *lead* the way.
	(noun) when pronounced as "led" it is a metal
	The building is reinforced with *lead*.
led	(verb) past tense of "to lead"
	Last night he *led* the team to victory.
learn	(verb) to acquire knowledge
teach	(verb) to instruct
	Test how well you have *learned* something by *teaching* it to someone else.
leave	(verb) to depart from
	We must *leave* soon to get to the show on time.
	(noun) permission to be absent
	The soldier is on *leave* for three weeks.
let	(verb) to permit
	Emma's parents *let* her go to the movies with us.
loose	(adjective) free, not close together (rhymes with "moose")
	The child's *loose* tooth fell out.

lose   (verb) to suffer loss (rhymes with "fuse")
Never *lose* your sense of humor.

moral   (noun) having to do with good or right; a lesson of conduct
Fables are stories that teach *morals*.
morale   (noun) mental condition, spirit
The failing grade had an adverse effect on the student's *morale*.

passed   (verb) the past tense of "pass"
He *passed* his chemistry test.
past   (can be used as noun, adjective or preposition) gone by, ended
The *past* has a way of influencing the future. A psychiatrist encourages his patients to recall their *past* experiences. He ran *past* us on the track.

peace   (noun) harmony; freedom from war
There was only a short period of *peace* between the end of World War II and the Korean War.
piece   (noun) a part of something
Please cut me a *piece* of pie.

plain   (noun) a flat area of land; clearly seen or understood
People who populate the *plains* are familiar with tornados.
It is *plain* to me that you want the job.
(adjective) not fancy
John wears *plain* clothes.
plane   (noun) a flat surface used mainly in geometry; an airplane; a tool used to smooth the surface of wood
Two non-intersecting lines in the same *plane* are parallel.
My *plane* is scheduled to depart in an hour.
The carpenter used a *plane* to smooth the wood.

principal   (noun) the head of a school
The *principal* of our school addressed the parents.
(adjective) primary, most important
The teacher's *principal* goal is to teach the children self-respect.
principle   (noun) an idea; a rule of conduct; a law; a main fact
Americans live by certain *principles*.
The *principles* of physics are fun to prove.

quiet	(adjective) silent, still
	Toddlers need a *quiet* time each day.
quit	(verb) to stop
	He *quit* his job to attend college.
quite	(adverb) to a great extent or degree; completely
	Maria is *quite* sure that she will win the race.

raise	(verb) to lift or elevate (has a direct object)
	The children *raise* their hands if they know the answer.
rise	(verb) to get up from a lying, sitting, or kneeling position
	How early do you *rise* in the morning?
rays	(noun) thin beams of light
	Rays of sunlight filtered through the blinds.
raze	(verb) to tear down completely
	The abandoned building was *razed* to build the mall.

shone	(verb) past tense of "shine"
	The sun *shone* brightly this morning.
shown	(verb) past tense of "show"
	Gina has not *shown* her parents her report card.

sit	(verb) to place the body in a seated position
	Please *sit* and wait your turn.
set	(verb) to place (followed by noun)
	Please help me *set* the table.

stationary	(adjective) in a fixed position
	The furniture on the boat is *stationary* to keep it from shifting.
stationery	(noun) writing paper
	Mom uses engraved *stationery* to write thank you notes.

than	(conjunction) used for comparisons
	My sister is younger *than* I.
then	(adverb or conjunction) indicates "at that time" or "next"
	Did you know them *then*?
	I did my chores; *then* I watched TV.

their	(possessive pronoun) must be followed by a noun
	This is *their* home.
there	(adverb) used to point out a location

	Place these books *there* on the shelf.
they're	(contraction) for "they are"
	They're our friends.
threw	(verb) past tense of "throw"
	The boys *threw* snowballs at the passing cars.
through	(preposition) passing from one side to another
	The students walked *through* the halls quietly.
to	(preposition) in the direction of
	We went *to* the game.
too	(adverb) very or many; also
	He went to the game, *too*.
	It was *too* cold to go swimming.
two	(adjective) refers to the number
	Those *two* girl are good friends.
ware	(noun) a product that is sold
	The salesman sold his *wares* door to door.
wear	(verb) to have on or to carry on one's body
	The little girl wanted to *wear* her new dress to the party.
where	(adverb) in or at what place
	Where do you want to live?
weather	(noun) the condition of the atmosphere
	The *weather* can be unpredictable.
whether	(conjunction) used to introduce the first of two or more alternatives
	You must decide *whether* to fly or to take the train.
who's	(contraction) for "who is"
	Who's the leader of the group?
whose	(possessive pronoun) must be followed by a noun
	Whose toys are these?
your	(possessive pronoun) must be followed by a noun
	Is this *your* book?
you're	(contraction) for "you are"
	You're my best friend.

Appendix 4A

1. The <u>most successful</u> athletes, <u>regardless of</u> the sport in which they excel, <u>is</u> always
         A   B   C

    striving to improve <u>their</u> performance. <u>No error</u>
                    D   E

2. *Gulliver's Travels*, the <u>timeless novel</u> by Jonathan Swift, <u>continue to captivate</u>
                         A   B   C

    <u>readers of all ages</u>. <u>No error</u>
        D   E

3. Pollen and ragweed, <u>abundant</u> in spring and early summer, <u>causes</u> many
                     A   B

    individuals <u>to suffer</u> allergic <u>reactions</u>. <u>No error</u>
            C   D   E

4. <u>No matter</u> when the immigrants came or what <u>their</u> country of origin <u>is</u>, the
      A   B   C

    newcomers were happy to have reached their <u>adopted</u> country. <u>No error</u>
                                          D   E

5. <u>Because</u> the storm had made access to the main road impossible, the children <u>seek</u>
      A   B

    refuge in the barn of the <u>neighboring</u> farm. <u>No error</u>
      C   D   E

6. <u>As the jury</u> entered the packed courtroom with <u>their</u> verdict, the defendant
      A   B

    <u>anxiously</u> awaited her <u>fate</u>. <u>No error</u>
       C   D   E

7. <u>Each of the contestants</u> secretly hoped <u>he</u> would be selected <u>to advance</u> to the
      A   B   C   D

    final round. <u>No error</u>
               E

8. <u>Everyone</u> of the players <u>entering</u> the stadium <u>was required</u> <u>to show</u> identification at
      A   B   C   D

    the main gate. <u>No error</u>.
                E

9. <u>Both</u> Laura and Ashley, best friends <u>since</u> childhood, received <u>a scholarship</u> from
      A   B   C

    Columbia University based on <u>their</u> academic excellence. <u>No error</u>
                               D   E

10. Chaz and Derrick, <u>avid baseball</u> fans, waited <u>on line</u> for two days <u>to purchase</u>
                     A   B   C

    <u>a ticket</u> to the first game of the World Series. <u>No error</u>
      D   E

11. The twins, for <u>who</u> the surprise party <u>was given,</u> <u>happily</u> greeted <u>their</u> friends and
               A   B   C   D

    relatives. <u>No error</u>
              E

12. <u>Between</u> you and <u>I,</u> Tom is the <u>best</u> candidate <u>for</u> senior class president. <u>No error</u>
     A   B   C   D   E

13. <u>Everyone</u> of <u>her friends,</u> except Jane and <u>I,</u> <u>was invited</u> to Susan's graduation party.
      A   B   C   D

   <u>No error</u>
      E

14. The boss was <u>angry at</u> many of <u>his</u> employees for both <u>their</u> lack of initiative and
                   A   B   C

    their <u>frequent</u> tardiness. <u>No error</u>
         D   E

15. The <u>students'</u> views <u>differ than</u> <u>those</u> of the administration <u>concerning</u> a dress code.
      A   B   C   D

   <u>No error</u>
      E

16. The class project <u>was</u> to compare the sitcoms of the <u>fifties</u> <u>to</u> the sitcoms <u>of today.</u>
                  A   B   C   D

   <u>No error</u>
      E

17. The <u>award winning</u> swimmer attributed <u>her success</u> to an exercise regimen, a twice
         A   B

    daily practice schedule, <u>and</u> <u>maintaining a positive attitude.</u> <u>No error</u>
                            C   D   E

18. The water enthusiast <u>not only enjoyed water skiing but also speed boat racing.</u>

    a) not only enjoyed water skiing but also speed boat racing.
    b) enjoyed not only water skiing but also speed boat racing.
    c) not only enjoyed water skiing and also speed boat racing.
    d) not only enjoyed water skiing but racing speed boats.

19. The hurricane tore through the village, flooding streets, <u>washing away trees and
    roads were made impassable.</u>

    a) washing away trees and roads were made impassable.
    b) washed away the trees and made the roads impassable.
    c) washed away the trees, making the roads impassable.
    d) washing away trees and making roads impassable.

20. The <u>distraught</u> mother <u>anxiously</u> watched as her young child sat <u>calm</u> allowing
            A   B   C

   the doctor to stitch his <u>badly</u> cut finger. <u>No error</u>
                          D   E

21. The <u>lovely</u> young woman <u>approached</u> the <u>hassled</u> clerk and <u>quiet</u> asked for a refund.
          A   B   C   D
   <u>No error</u>
     E

22. <u>The evening news commentator is much more formal than the morning news.</u>

   a) The evening news commentator is much more formal than the morning news.
   b) The commentator for the evening news is much more formal than the morning news.
   c) The evening news commentator is much more formal than the morning news commentator.
   d) The commentator of the evening news is a lot more formal than the morning news.

23. <u>My friend Mark is taller than any of the players on his basketball team.</u>

   a) My friend Mark is taller than any of the players on his basketball team.
   b) My friend Mark is taller than any of the other players on his basketball team.
   c) My friend Mark tallest of the players on his basketball team.
   d) Mark my friend is taller than any of the players on his basketball team.

24. My kitten is <u>quicker</u> <u>than</u> my puppy, <u>but</u> my puppy is <u>strongest</u>. <u>No error</u>
         A   B   C   D   E

25. The new dining room set <u>and</u> rug <u>were</u> delivered, but <u>it</u> was <u>noticeably</u> damaged.
                    A   B   C   D

   <u>No error</u>
      E

26. <u>It</u> <u>was</u> a great day for the beach, <u>so</u> I called my friends, Mary and Jean, but <u>she</u>
   A   B   C   D
   didn't answer. <u>No error</u>
                     E

27. The novels of James Patterson <u>are</u> more realistic and <u>more</u> terrifying <u>than</u>
                              A   B   C

   <u>Mary Higgins Clark.</u>   <u>No error</u>
         D   E

28. <u>At the age of ninety, my father took his first Caribbean cruise; and he enjoyed every minute of it.</u>

   a) At the age of ninety, my father took his first Caribbean cruise; and he enjoyed every minute of it.
   b) At the age of ninety, my father's first Caribbean cruise was taken by him; and he enjoyed every minute of it.
   c) At ninety, my father took his first Caribbean cruise; he enjoyed every minute of it.
   d) At ninety, my father took his first Caribbean cruise he enjoyed every minute of it.

29. The season of spring triggers allergy symptoms in many people. No error
        A   B   C   D   E

30. Susan liked to read historical novels of which she found those dealing with the era of the Civil War more interesting than any others.

a) novels of which she found those dealing with the era of the Civil War more interesting than any others.
b) novels, about the era of the Civil War was the most interesting.
c) novels, she found those dealing with the era of the Civil War the most interesting.
d) novels; she found those dealing with the era of the Civil War the most interesting.

Appendix 4D

31. <u>The term paper is still on my desk that should have been turned in yesterday</u>.

    a) The term paper is still on my desk that should have been turned in yesterday.
    b) The term paper that should have been turned in yesterday is still on my desk.
    c) The term paper is still on my desk, while it should have been turned in yesterday.
    d) The term paper is still on my desk, it should have been turned in yesterday

32. <u>My two pit bulls frightened the thief away barking and growling</u>.
    a) My two pit bulls frightened the thief away barking and growling.
    b) My two pit bulls were barking and growling, the thief was frightened away.
    c) My two pit bulls, barking and growling, frightened the thief away.
    d) My two pit bulls, barking and growling, frightening the thief away.

33. <u>Slamming on the brakes</u>, the car slid across the icy road and broke through the guard rail.
    a) Slamming on the brakes,
    b) As the brakes were being slammed on,
    c) The brakes having been slammed by me,
    d) When I slammed on the brakes,

34. Recognizing the errors of his ways, <u>that his parents did not accept his sincere change of heart upset the boy</u>.

    a) that his parents did not accept his sincere change of heart upset the boy.

    b) his sincere change of heart was not accepted by his parents.

    c) the boy was upset when his parents did not accept his sincere change of heart.

    d) his parents refusal to accept his sincere change of heart upset him.

35. The <u>counselor</u> gave erroneous <u>advise</u> <u>concerning</u> the <u>requirements for</u> the available
        A   B   C   D
    position. <u>No error</u>
             E

36. We <u>don't</u> never go to a professional football game, <u>except</u> when my grandfather <u>visits</u>
        A   B   C
    <u>us</u>. <u>No error</u>
    D   E

Appendix 4E

37.   American students <u>that</u> travel overseas <u>should become</u> familiar with the laws of
                            A   B
       the country <u>they</u> <u>are</u> visiting. <u>No error</u>
                     C   D   E

38.   The <u>class</u> <u>which</u> <u>sells</u> the most raffle tickets <u>earns</u> a pizza party.
             A   B   C   D
       <u>No error</u>
           E

39.   <u>If</u> you want to be successful, <u>one</u> must be willing <u>to learn</u> from <u>your</u> mistakes.
         A   B   C   D
       <u>No error</u>
           E

40.   The scenery along the mountain roads <u>was particularly spectacular at sunset it</u>
       <u>begged to be photographed.</u>

       a) was particularly spectacular at sunset it begged to be photographed.
       b) was spectacular particular at sunset; it begged to be photographed.
       c) was particularly spectacular at sunset; it begged to be photographed.
       d) were particularly spectacular at sunset; they begged to be photographed.

41.   <u>Aided by a group of teachers whom he alternately praised and demeaned.</u>

       a) Aided by a group of teachers whom he alternately praised and demeaned.
       b) He, aided by a group of teachers, whom he alternately praised and demeaned.
       c) He, who was aided by a group of teachers, whom he alternately praised and
          demeaned.
       d) He was aided by a group of teachers whom he alternately praised and
          demeaned.

42.   Susan would like to tour the British Isles this summer, <u>but she cannot afford to do so.</u>

       a) but she cannot afford to do so.
       b) and she could not afford to do so.
       c) but this trip was not affordable by her.
       d) but she could not afford the expenses of such a trip.

43.   <u>The homes in most of the villages were destroyed by the powerful earthquake.</u>

       a) The homes in most of the village were destroyed by the powerful earthquake.
       b) The homes in most of the village was destroyed by the powerful earthquake.
       c) The powerful earthquake destroyed most of the homes in the village.
       d) Most of the village homes were destroyed by the powerful earthquake.

Answer Key-Practice Sentences

Appendix 4A

1. C are
2. B continues
3. B cause
4. C was
5. B sought
6. B its
7. E
8. E
9. C scholarships
10.D tickets

Appendix 4B

11. A whom
12. B me
13. C me
14. A angry with-idiom
15. B differ from–idiom
16. C compare with-idiom
17. D a positive attitude – parallel structure
18. B correlative conjunctions precede parallel terms
19. D parallel structure
20. C calmly
21. D quietly

Appendix 4C

22. C apples and oranges
23. B comparison
24. D stronger
25. C "it" is ambiguous
26. D "she" can refer to Mary or Jean
27. D apples and oranges
28. C wordiness
29. A wordiness
30. D wordiness

Appendix 4D

31. B misplaced modifier
32. C misplaced modifier
33. D dangling modifier
34. C misplaced modifier
35. B advice – words commonly confused
36. A double negative

Appendix 4E

37. A who
38. B that
39. B you
40. C run-on
41. D fragment
42. A active voice + correct conjunction "but," not "and"
43. C Choose active voice over passive voice when given a choice; passive voice is always wordier.

Made in the USA
Charleston, SC
18 April 2011